Animals I Will Find at the Zoo
SUN BEAR

Shannon Anderson

Table of Contents

SUN BEAR...3
WORDS TO KNOW......................................22
INDEX 23
COMPREHENSION QUESTIONS 23
ABOUT THE AUTHOR...................................24

A Starfish Book

Teaching Tips for Caregivers:

As a caregiver, you can help your child succeed in school by giving them a strong foundation in language and literacy skills and a desire to learn to read.

This book helps children grow by letting them practice reading skills.

Reading for pleasure and interest will help your child to develop reading skills and will give your child the opportunity to practice these skills in meaningful ways.

- Encourage your child to read on her own at home
- Encourage your child to practice reading aloud
- Encourage activities that require reading
- Establish a reading time
- Talk with your child
- Give your child writing materials

Teaching Tips for Teachers:

Research shows that one of the best ways for students to learn a new topic is to read about it.

Before Reading

- Read the "Words to Know" and discuss the meaning of each word.
- Read the back cover to see what the book is about.

During Reading

- When a student gets to a word that is unknown, ask them to look at the rest of the sentence to find clues to help with the meaning of the unknown word.
- Ask the student to write down any pages of the book that were confusing to them.

After Reading

- Discuss the main idea of the book.
- Ask students to give one detail that they learned in the book by showing a text dependent answer from the book.

SUN BEAR

A zoo is a fun place to see animals and learn about them.

One animal you may find in a zoo is a sun bear.

Sun bears are the smallest of all bears.

They got their name from the golden patch of fur on their chest.

Sun bears have long claws for digging and climbing.

Their tongues are super long!

Their tongues help them get honey from beehives and **termites** from trees.

Sun bear claws are four inches (10 centimeters) long. Sun bear tongues are ten inches (25 centimeters) long.

Sun bears are **omnivores**.

Besides honey, they eat fruit, insects, and small animals.

At night, sun bears hunt for food.

In the daytime, they spend a lot of time sleeping.

Baby sun bears are called cubs.

Most moms have only one cub at a time.

Cubs start learning to climb trees when they are two months old.

Sun bears are **mammals**, so cubs drink their mom's milk for about four months.

Cubs stay with their moms for at least two years.

Sun bears can live to be 25 years old.

There are not many sun bears left in the world.

Sun bears are shy. They try to stay away from people.

People hunting and cutting down trees make it hard for sun bears to survive.

New laws protect sun bears from being hunted.

Sun bears live in **Asia** in the **rainforest**.

If you cannot go to Asia to see sun bears, you can find them at the zoo!

Words to Know

Asia (AY-zhuh): one of Earth's continents; a very large land mass in the eastern hemisphere north of the equator

mammals (MAM-uhlz): animals that have hair or fur, that give birth to live babies, and that make milk to feed their babies

omnivores (AHM-nuh-vors): animals that eat both plants and meat

rainforest (RAYN-for-ist): a forest in a tropical region of the world where it rains a lot

termites (TUR-mites): small, ant-like insects that eat wood

Index

Asia 20, 21
baby/cubs 12, 13, 15
eat 9
fur 4
laws 19
tongues 6, 7

Comprehension Questions

1. Why are these bears called sun bears?
    a. They love to be in the sunshine.
    b. They are bright yellow.
    c. They have a patch of golden fur on their chest.

2. What do sun bears like to eat?
    a. fruit and small animals
    b. tree bark
    c. deer and antelope

3. Baby sun bears are called ___.
    a. kits   b. cubs   c. pups

4. True or False: A sun bear's tongue is longer than its claws.

5. True or False: There are a huge number of sun bears in the world.

Answers
1. c 2. a 3. b 4. True 5. False

About the Author

Shannon Anderson is an award-winning children's book author and former elementary school teacher. She loves animals and has eight pets of her own. You can learn more about her or invite her to your school at www.shannonisteaching.com.

Written by: Shannon Anderson
Design by: Under the Oaks Media
Editor: Kim Thompson

Photographs/Shutterstock: Yatra4289: cover, p. 7; Cuson: p. 3; Ross Gordon Henry: p. 5; CelsoDiniz: p. 8; GuitarStudio: p. 10-11; AndrewLilly: p. 13; Arief Budi Kusuma: p. 14; Benzine: p. 17; Abdelrahman Hassanein: p. 18; Pyty: p. 20 (map); Tigerstocks: p. 20; Apiwich Pudsimian: p. 21

Library of Congress PCN Data
Sun Bear / Shannon Anderson
Animals I Will Find at the Zoo
ISBN 979-8-8873-5350-0 (hard cover)
ISBN 979-8-8873-5435-4 (paperback)
ISBN 979-8-8873-5520-7 (EPUB)
ISBN 979-8-8873-5605-1 (eBook)
Library of Congress Control Number: 2022949031

Printed in the United States of America.

Seahorse Publishing Company
www.seahorsepub.com

Copyright © 2024 **SEAHORSE PUBLISHING COMPANY**

All rights reserved. No part of this publication may be reproduced, stored in a retrieval system or be transmitted in any form or by any means, electronic, mechanical, photocopying, recording, or otherwise, without the prior written permission of Seahorse Publishing Company.

Published in the United States
Seahorse Publishing
PO Box 771325
Coral Springs, FL 33077